Homage to
MISTRESS
BRADSTREET

By John Berryman

With Pictures by BEN SHAHN

New York · FARRAR, STRAUS & GIROUX

© 1956 by John Berryman
Library of Congress
catalog card number 56-6168

First printing, 1956
Second printing, 1964
Third printing, 1967

Published simultaneously in Canada
by Ambassador Books, Ltd., Toronto.
Manufactured in the U. S. A.

The author wishes to record his deep gratefulness to Mr Moe and others for the Guggenheim fellowship which let this work be finished; and to friends; acknowledgment is made also to the editors of Partisan Review *where it first appeared, and to a correspondent who supplied some of the notes at the end.*

Homage to
MISTRESS
BRADSTREET

[Born 1612 Anne Dudley, married at
16 Simon Bradstreet, a Cambridge
man, steward to the Countess of War-
wick & protégé of her father Thomas
Dudley secretary to the Earl of Lin-
coln. Crossed in the *Arbella*, 1630,
under Governor Winthrop.]

Homage to
MISTRESS
BRADSTREET

. . . **1**

The Governor your husband lived so long
moved you not, restless, waiting for him? Still,
you were a patient woman. —
I seem to see you pause here still:
Sylvester, Quarles, in moments odd you pored
before a fire at, bright eyes on the Lord,
all the children still.
'Simon . .' Simon will listen while you read a Song.

Outside the New World winters in grand dark
white air lashing high thro' the virgin stands
foxes down foxholes sigh,
surely the English heart quails, stunned.
I doubt if Simon than this blast, that sea,
spares from his rigour for your poetry
more. We are on each other's hands
who care. Both of our worlds unhanded us. Lie stark,

thy eyes look to me mild. Out of maize & air
your body's made, and moves. I summon, see,
from the centuries it.
I think you won't stay. How do we
linger, diminished, in our lovers' air,
implausibly visible, to whom, a year,
years, over interims; or not;
to a long stranger; or not; shimmer & disappear.

Jaw-ript, rot with its wisdom, rending then;
then not. When the mouth dies, who misses you?
Your master never died,
Simon ah thirty years past you —
Pockmarkt & westward staring on a haggard deck
it seems I find you, young. I come to check,
I come to stay with you,
and the Governor, & Father, & Simon, & the huddled
     men.

By the week we landed we were, most, used up.
Strange ships across us, after a fortnight's winds
unfavouring, frightened us;
bone-sad cold, sleet, scurvy; so were ill
many as one day we could have no sermons;
broils, quelled; a fatherless child unkennelled; vermin
crowding & waiting: waiting.
And the day itself he leapt ashore young Henry
     Winthrop

(delivered from the waves; because he found
off their wigwams, sharp-eyed, a lone canoe
across a tidal river,
that water glittered fair & blue
& narrow, none of the other men could swim
and the plantation's prime theft up to him,
shouldered on a glad day
hard on the glorious feasting of thanksgiving)
    drowned.

How long with nothing in the ruinous heat,
clams & acorns stomaching, distinction perishing,
at which my heart rose,
with brackish water, we would sing.
When whispers knew the Governor's last bread
was browning in his oven, we were discourag'd.
The Lady Arbella dying —
dyings — at which my heart   rose, but I did submit.

That beyond the Atlantic wound our woes enlarge
is hard, hard that starvation burnishes our fear,
but I do gloss for You.
Strangers & pilgrims fare we here,
declaring we seek a City. Shall we be deceived?
I know whom I have trusted, & whom I have believed,
and that he is able to
keep   that I have committed to his charge.

Winter than summer worse, that first, like a file
on a quick, or the poison suck of a thrilled tooth;
and still we may unpack.
Wolves & storms among, uncouth
board-pieces, boxes, barrels vanish, grow
houses, rise. Motes that hop in sunlight slow
indoors, and I am Ruth
away: open my mouth, my eyes wet: I wóuld smile:

vellum I palm, and dream. Their forest dies
to greensward, privets, elms & towers, whence
a nightingale is throbbing.
Women sleep sound. I was happy once . .
(Something keeps on not happening; I shrink?)
These minutes all their passions & powers sink
and I am not one chance
for an unknown cry or a flicker of unknown eyes.

Chapped souls ours, by the day Spring's strong winds
        swelled,
Jack's pulpits arched, more glad. The shawl I pinned
flaps like a shooting soul
might in such weather Heaven send.
Succumbing half, in spirit, to a salmon sash
I prod the nerveless novel succotash —
I must be disciplined,
in arms, against that one, and our dissidents, and
        myself.

Versing, I shroud among the dynasties;
quaternion on quaternion, tireless I phrase
anything past, dead, far,
sacred, for a barbarous place.
—To please your wintry father? all this bald
abstract didactic rime I read appalled
harassed for your fame
mistress neither of fiery nor velvet verse, on your
    knees

hopeful & shamefast, chaste, laborious, odd,
whom the sea tore. —The damned roar with loss,
so they hug & are mean
with themselves, and I cannot be thus.
Why then do I repine, sick, bad, to long
after what must not be? I lie wrong
once more. For at fourteen
I found my heart more carnal and sitting loose from
    God,

vanity & the follies of youth took hold of me;
then the pox blasted, when the Lord returned.
That year for my sorry face
so-much-older Simon burned,
so Father smiled, with love. Their will be done.
He to me ill lingeringly, learning to shun
a bliss, a lightning blood
vouchsafed, what did seem life. I kissed his Mystery.

Drydust in God's eye the aquavivid skin
of Simon snoring lit with fountaining dawn
when my eyes unlid, sad.
John Cotton shines on Boston's sin —
I ám drawn, in pieties that seem
the weary drizzle of an unremembered dream.
Women have gone mad
at twenty-one. Ambition mines, atrocious, in.

Food endless, people few, all to be done.
As pippins roast, the question of the wolves
turns & turns.
Fangs of a wolf will keep, the neck
round of a child, that child brave. I remember who
in meeting smiled & was punisht, and I know who
whispered & was stockt.
We lead a thoughtful life. But Boston's cage we shun.

The winters close, Springs open, no child stirs
under my withering heart, O seasoned heart
God grudged his aid.
All things else soil like a shirt.
Simon is much away. My executive stales.
The town came through for the cartway by the pales,
but my patience is short.
I revolt from, I am like, these savage foresters

whose passionless dicker in the shade, whose glance
impassive & scant, belie their murderous cries
when quarry seems to show.
Again I must have been wrong, twice.
Unwell in a new way. Can that begin?
God brandishes. O love, O I love. Kin,
gather. My world is strange
and merciful, ingrown months, blessing a swelling
      trance.

So squeezed, wince you I scream? I love you & hate
off with you. Ages! *Useless*. Below my waist
he has me in Hell's vise.
Stalling. He let go. Come back: brace
me somewhere. No. No. Yes! everything down
hardens I press with horrible joy down
my back cracks like a wrist
shame I am voiding oh behind it is too late

hide me forever I work thrust I must free
now I all muscles & bones concentrate
what is living from dying?
Simon I must leave you so untidy
Monster you are killing me Be sure
I'll have you later Women do endure
I can *can* no longer
and it passes the wretched trap whelming and I am me

drencht & powerful, I did it with my body!
One proud tug greens Heaven. Marvellous,
unforbidding Majesty.
Swell, imperious bells. I fly.
Mountainous, woman not breaks and will bend:
sways God nearby: anguish comes to an end.
Blossomed Sarah, and I
blossom. Is that thing alive? I hear a famisht howl.

Beloved household, I am Simon's wife,
and the mother of Samuel — whom greedy yet I miss
out of his kicking place.
More in some ways I feel at a loss,
freer. Cantabanks & mummers, nears
longing for you. Our chopping scores my ears,
our costume bores my eyes.
St. George to the good sword, rise! chop-logic's rife

& fever & Satan & Satan's ancient fere.
Pioneering is not feeling well,
not Indians, beasts.
Not all their riddling can forestall
one leaving. Sam, your uncle has had to
go fróm us to live with God. 'Then Aunt went too?'
Dear, she does wait still.
Stricken: 'Oh. Then he takes   us one by one.' My dear.

Forswearing it otherwise, they starch their minds.
Folkmoots, & blether, blether. John Cotton rakes
to the synod of Cambridge.
Down from my body my legs flow,
out from it arms wave, on it my head shakes.
Now Mistress Hutchinson rings forth a call —
should she? many creep out at a broken wall —
affirming the Holy Ghost
dwells in one justified. Factioning passion blinds

all to all her good, all — can she be exiled?
Bitter sister, victim! I miss you.
— I miss you, Anne,
day or night weak as a child,
tender & empty, doomed, quick to no tryst.
— I hear you. Be kind, you who leaguer
my image in the mist.
— Be kind you, to one unchained eager far & wild

and if, O my love, my heart is breaking, please
neglect my cries and I will spare you. Deep
in Time's grave, Love's, you lie still.
Lie still. — Now? That happy shape
my forehead had under my most long, rare,
ravendark, hidden, soft bodiless hair
you award me still.
You must not love me, but   I do not bid you cease.

Veiled my eyes, attending. How can it be I?
Moist, with parted lips, I listen, wicked.
I shake in the morning & retch.
Brood I do on myself naked.
A fading world I dust, with fingers new.
— I have earned the right to be alone with you.
—What right can that be?
Convulsing, if you love, enough, like a sweet lie.

Not that, I know, you can. This cratered skin,
like the crabs & shells of my Palissy ewer, touch!
Oh, you do, you do?
Falls on me what I like a witch,
for lawless holds, annihilations of law
which Time and he and man abhor, foresaw:
sharper than what my Friend
brought me for my revolt when I moved smooth &
 thin,

faintings black, rigour, chilling, brown
parching, back, brain burning, the grey pocks
itch, a manic stench
of pustules snapping, pain floods the palm,
sleepless, or a red shaft with a dreadful start
rides at the chapel, like a slipping heart.
My soul strains in one qualm
ah but *this* is not to save me but to throw me down.

And out of this I lull. It lessens. Kiss me.
That once. As sings out up in sparkling dark
a trail of a star & dies,
while the breath flutters, sounding, mark,
so shorn ought such caresses to us be
who, deserving nothing, flush and flee
the darkness of that light,
a lurching frozen from a warm dream. Talk to me.

— It is Spring's New England. Pussy willows wedge
up in the wet. Milky crestings, fringed
yellow, in heaven, eyed
by the melting hand-in-hand or mere
desirers single, heavy-footed, rapt,
make surge poor human hearts. Venus is trapt —
the hefty pike shifts, sheer —
in Orion blazing. Warblings, odours, nudge to an
    edge—

— Ravishing, ha, what crouches outside ought,
flamboyant, ill, angelic. Often, now,
I am afraid of you.
I am a sobersides; I know.
I *want* to take you for my lover. — Do.
— I hear a madness. Harmless I to you
am not, not I? — No.
— I cannot but be. Sing a concord of our thought.

—Wan dolls in indigo on gold: refrain
my western lust. I am drowning in this past.
I lose sight of you
who mistress me from air. Unbraced
in delirium of the grand depths, giving away
haunters what kept me, I breathe solid spray.
— I am losing you!
Straiten me on. — I suffered living like a stain:

I trundle the bodies, on the iron bars,
over that fire backward & forth; they burn;
bits fall. I wonder if
I killed them. Women serve my turn.
— Dreams! You are good. — No. — Dense with
　　hardihood
the wicked are dislodged, and lodged the good.
In green space we are safe.
God awaits us (but I　am yielding) who Hell wars.

— I cannot feel myself God waits. He flies
nearer a kindly world; or he is flown.
One Saturday's rescue
won't show. Man is entirely alone
may be. I am a man of griefs & fits
trying to be my friend. And the brown smock splits,
down the pale flesh a gash
broadens and Time holds up your heart against my
　　eyes.

— Hard and divided heaven! creases me. Shame
is failing. My breath is scented, and I throw
hostile glances towards God.
Crumpling plunge of a pestle, bray:
sin cross & opposite, wherein I survive
nightmares of Eden. Reaches foul & live
he for me, this soul
to crunch, a minute tangle of eternal flame.

I fear Hell's hammer-wind. But fear does wane.
Death's blossoms grain my hair; I cannot live.
A black joy clashes
joy, in twilight. The Devil said
'I will deal toward her softly, and her enchanting
     cries
will fool the horns of Adam.' Father of lies,
a male great pestle smashes
small women swarming towards the mortar's rim
     in vain.

I see the cruel spread Wings black with saints!
Silky my breasts not his, mine, mine to withhold
or tender, tender.
I am sifting, nervous, and bold.
The light is changing. Surrender this loveliness
you cannot make me do. *But* I will. Yes.
What horror, down stormy air,
warps towards me? My threatening promise faints —

torture me, Father, lest not I be thine!
Tribunal terrible & pure, my God,
mercy for him and me.
Faces half-fanged, Christ drives abroad,
and though the crop hopes, Jane is so slipshod
I cry. Evil dissolves, & love, like foam;
that love. Prattle of children powers me home,
my heart claps like the swan's
under a frenzy of *who* love me & who shine.

As a canoe slides by on one strong stroke
hope his hélp not I, who do hardly bear
his gift still. But whisper
I am not utterly. I pare
an apple for my pipsqueak Mercy and
she runs & all need naked apples, fanned
their tinier envies.
Vomitings, trots, rashes. Can be hope a cloak?

for the man with cropt ears glares. My fingers tighten
my skirt. I pass. Alas! I pity all.
Shy, shy, with mé, Dorothy.
Moonrise, and frightening hoots. 'Mother,
how *long* will I be dead?' Our friend the owl
vanishes, darling, but your homing soul
retires on Heaven, Mercy:
not we one instant die, only our dark does lighten.

When by me in the dusk my child sits down
I am myself. Simon, if it's that loose,
let me wiggle it out.
You'll get a bigger one there, & bite.
How they loft, how their sizes delight and grate.
The proportioned, spiritless poems accumulate.
And they publish them
away in brutish London, for a hollow crown.

Father is not himself. He keeps his bed,
and threw a saffron scum Thursday. God-forsaken
     words
escaped him raving. Save,
Lord, thy servant zealous & just.
Sam he saw back from Harvard. He did scold
his secting enemies. His stomach is cold
while we drip, while
my baby John breaks out. O far from where he bred!

Bone of moaning: sung Where he has gone
a thousand summers by truth-hallowed souls;
be still. Agh, he is gone!
Where? I know. Beyond the shoal.
Still-all a Christian daughter grinds her teeth
a little. This our land has ghosted with
our dead: I am at home.
Finish, Lord, in me this work thou hast begun.

And they tower, whom the pear-tree lured
to let them fall, fierce mornings they reclined
down the brook-bank to the east
fishing for shiners with a crookt pin,
wading, dams massing, well, and Sam's to be
a doctor in Boston. After the divisive sea,
and death's first feast,
and the galled effort on the wilderness endured,

Arminians, and the King bore against us;
of an 'inward light' we hear with horror.
Whose fan is in his hand
and he will throughly purge his floor,
come towards mé. I have what licks the joints
and bites the heart, which winter more appoints.
Iller I, oftener.
Hard at the outset; in the ending thus hard, thus?

Sacred & unutterable Mind
flashing thorough the universe one thought,
I do wait without peace.
In the article of death I budge.
Eat my sore breath, Black Angel. Let me die.
Body a-drain, when will you be dry
and countenance my speed
to Heaven's springs? lest stricter writhings have me
        declined.

'What are those pictures in the air at night,
Mother?' Mercy did ask. Space charged with faces
day & night! I place
a goatskin's fetor, and sweat: fold me
in savoury arms. Something is shaking, wrong.
He smells the musket and lifts it. It is long.
It points at my heart.
Missed he must have. In the gross storm of sunlight

I sniff a fire burning without outlet,
consuming acrid its own smoke. It's me.
Ruined laughter sounds
outside. Ah but I waken, free.
And so I am about again. I hagged
a fury at the short maid, whom tongues tagged,
and I am sorry. Once
less I was anxious when more passioned to upset

the mansion & the garden & the beauty of God.
Insectile unreflective busyness
blunts & does amend.
Hangnails, piles, fibs, life's also.
But we are that from which draws back a thumb.
The seasons stream and, somehow, I am become
an old woman. It's so:
I look. I bear to look. Strokes once more his rod.

My window gives on the graves, in our great new
  house
(how many burned?) upstairs, among the elms.
I lie, & endure, & wonder.
A haze slips sometimes over my dreams
and holiness on horses' bells shall stand.
Wandering pacemaker, unsteadying friend,
in a redskin calm I wait:
beat when you will our end. Sinkings & droopings
  drowse.

Ben Shahn

They say thro' the fading winter Dorothy fails,
my second, who than I bore one more, nine;
and I see her inearthed. I linger.
Seaborn she wed knelt before Simon;
Simon I, and linger. Black-yellow seething, vast
it lies fróm me, mine: all they look aghast.
It will be a glorious arm.
Docile I watch. My wreckt chest hurts when Simon
        pales.

In the yellowing days your faces wholly fail,
at Fall's onset. Solemn voices fade.
I feel no coverlet.
Light notes leap, a beckon, swaying
the tilted, sickening ear within. I'll — I'll —
I am closed & coming. Somewhere! I defile
wide as a cloud, in a cloud,
unfit, desirous, glad — even the singings veil —

—You are not ready? You áre ready. Pass,
as shadow gathers shadow in the welling night.
Fireflies of childhood torch
you down. We commit our sister down.
One candle mourn by, which a lover gave,
the use's edge and order of her grave.
Quiet? Moisture shoots.
Hungry throngs collect. They sword into the carcass.

Headstones stagger under great draughts of time
after heads pass out, and their world must reel
speechless, blind in the end
about its chilling star: thrift tuft,
whin cushion — nothing. Already with the wounded
    flying
dark air fills, I am a closet of secrets dying,
races murder, foxholes hold men,
reactor piles wage slow upon the wet brain rime.

I must pretend to leave you. Only you draw off
a benevolent phantom. I say you seem to me
drowned towns off England,
featureless as those myriads
who what bequeathed save fire-ash, fossils, burled
in the open river-drifts of the Old World?
Simon lived on for years.
I renounce not even ragged glances, small teeth,
    nothing,

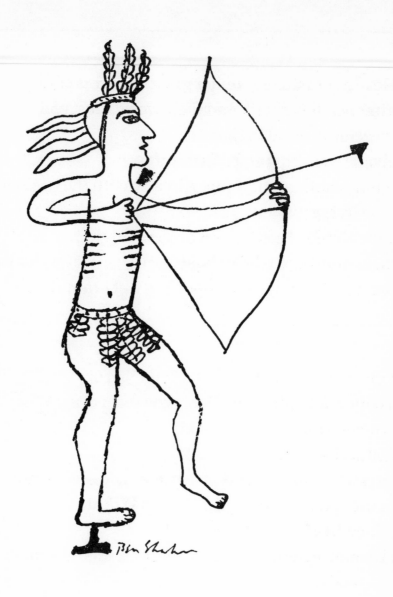

O all your ages at the mercy of my loves
together lie at once, forever or
so long as I happen.
In the rain of pain & departure, still
Love has no body and presides the sun,
and elfs from silence melody. I run.
Hover, utter, still,
a sourcing   whom my lost candle like the firefly loves.

Notes

Stanzas 1-4	The poem is about the woman but this exordium is spoken by the poet, his voice modulating in stanza 4, line 8 [4.8] into hers.
1.1	He was not Governor until after her death.
1.5	Sylvester (the translator of Du Bartas) and Quarles, her favourite poets; unfortunately.
5.4,5	Many details are from quotations in Helen Campbell's biography, the Winthrop papers, narratives, town histories.
8.4ff.	Scriptural passages are sometimes ones she used herself, as this in her *Meditation liii*.
11.8	*that one:* the Old One.
12.5-13.2	The poet interrupts.
18.8	Her first child was not born until about 1633.
22.6	*chopping:* disputing, snapping, haggling; axing.
23.1	*fere:* his friend Death.
24.1	Her irony of 22.8 intensifies.
24.2	*rakes:* inclines, as a mast; bows.
25.3	One might say: He is enabled to speak, at last, in the fortune of an echo of her — and when she is loneliest (her former spiritual

adviser having deserted Anne Hutchinson, and this her closest friend banished), as if she had summoned him; and only thus, perhaps, is she enabled to hear him. This second section of the poem is a dialogue, his voice however ceasing well before it ends at 39.4, and hers continuing for the whole third part, until the coda (54-57).

29.1-4   Cf. Isa. 1:5.

29.5,6   After a Klee.

33.1   Cf., on Byzantine icons, Frederick Rolfe ("Baron Corvo"): 'Who ever dreams of praying (with expectation of response) for the prayer of a Tintoretto or a Titian, or a Bellini, or a Botticelli? But who can refrain from crying "O Mother!" to these unruffleable wan dolls in indigo on gold?' (quoted from *The Desire and Pursuit of the Whole* by Graham Greene in *The Lost Childhood*).

33.5,6   'Délires des grandes profondeurs,' described by Cousteau and others; a euphoria, sometimes fatal, in which the hallucinated diver offers passing fish his line, helmet, anything.

35.3,4   As of cliffhangers, movie serials wherein each week's episode ends with a train bearing down on the strapped heroine or with the hero dangling over an abyss into which Indians above him peer with satisfaction before they hatchet the rope.

rescue: forcible recovery (by the owner) of goods distrained.

37.7,8	After an engraving somewhere in Fuchs's collections. *Bray*, above (36.4), puns.
39.5	The stanza is unsettled, like 24, by a middle line, signaling a broad transition.
42.8	*brutish:* her epithet for London in a kindly passage about the Great Fire.
46.1,2	Arminians, rebels against the doctrine of unconditional election. Her husband alone opposed the law condemning Quakers to death.
46.3,4	Matthew 3:12.
46.5,6	Rheumatic fever, after a celebrated French description.
48.2ff.	*Space . . . outside:* delirium.
51.5	Cf. Zech. 14:20.
51.6	*Wandering pacemaker:* a disease of the heart, here the heart itself.
52.4	Seaborn Cotton, John's eldest son; Bradstreet being then magistrate.
52.5,6	Dropsical, a complication of the last three years. Line 7 she actually said.
55.4	*thrift:* the plant, also called Our Lady's cushion.
55.8	*wet brain:* edema.
56.5,6	Cf. G. R. Levy, *The Gate of Horn*, p. 5.